I SLEEP

but my heart is

AWAKE

I SLEEP

but my heart is

AWAKE

a guided journal for

HEARING GOD THROUGH YOUR DREAMS

Stephanie Schureman

DESTINY IMAGE® PUBLISHERS, INC.
P.O. Box 310, Shippensburg, PA 17257-0310
"Promoting Inspired Lives."

This book and all other Destiny Image and Destiny Image Fiction books are available at Christian bookstores and distributors worldwide.

For more information on foreign distributors, call 717-532-3040.

Reach us on the Internet: www.destinyimage.com.

ISBN 13 TP: 978-0-7684-6369-9

For Worldwide Distribution, Printed in the U.S.A.

1 2 3 4 5 6 7 8 / 26 25 24 23 22

"[Daniel] could do anything—interpret dreams, solve mysteries, explain puzzles."

—Daniel 5:12, MSG

"The [Holy] Spirit...dives into the depths of God, and brings out what God planned all along. ...He [Holy Spirit] not only knows what he's [God is] thinking, but he lets us in on it. God offers a full report on the gifts of life and salvation that he is giving us. We don't have to rely on the world's guesses and opinions. We didn't learn this by reading books or going to school; we learned it from God, who taught us person-to-person through Jesus, and we're passing it on to you in the same firsthand, personal way."

—1 Corinthians 2:10-13, MSG

INTRODUCTION

Practical tips for journaling

1. Keep the journal and a pen beside your bed.

2. Write the dream as soon as possible. If you are awakened by a dream, even in the middle of the night, that is the time to write it down. It is risky to tell yourself you'll remember the dream in the morning. Dreams are quickly lost and when you wake you may have already forgotten the dream story. Recording your dreams takes some discipline, but you will be rewarded by the practice.

   My heart is on fire, boiling over with passion. Bubbling up within me are these beautiful lyrics as a lovely poem to be sung for the King. Like a river bursting its banks, I'm overflowing with words, spilling out into this sacred story (Psalm 45:1).

What about a digital voice recorder?

This works as well and is effective particularly if you dream a song, tune, rhythm, or other sound present in your dream. However, keeping a written copy is still important so that the dream is not lost if your device/recording becomes unavailable.

Keep your recording device handy. Make sure you can turn it on when sleepy and speak the dream clearly so you don't miss details. Recordings can be quite funny to hear in the morning.

What should I write down?

Write down the date of the dream and the approximate time you dreamed it. For instance, you may have a vague idea of the time— before midnight, after midnight, or around 4:00 a.m.

There are other times you'll remember exactly what time you woke from the dream because of the pattern of the numbers on the clock (such as 1:11, 3:16, 4:44, etc.).

What details are important?

Whatever stands out, is highlighted, or is impressed in your memory is worth writing down.

- Colors

- Numbers

- Is the dream dark or light?

- The story in the dream

- How did you feel in the dream?

Can I draw the dream?

Yes! Some dreams are best drawn or simply explained with lots of color or shapes.

Do I need to write the dream perfectly?

No, write the dream without concern for grammar or punctuation. The main goal is to get all the details of the dream written.

After writing the dream, ask Jesus for the interpretation.

You may already understand what the dream is, or you may have no idea. Write what you have, always asking Holy Spirit for more understanding.

Are dreams significant to God? Does He still speak to people in dreams? Is He speaking to you? If we look at all the biblical dreams, we see that there are 21. God used dreams to communicate many important events to our biblical forefathers. He even spoke to those who didn't love or serve him—Old Testament kings, the wise men from the East and Pontius Pilot's wife. Solomon received his wisdom gift from a dream. Jesus's earthly father received instruction not to hesitate to take Mary as his wife. He also received geographical guidance necessary to protect baby Jesus from being killed by Herod. There are dreams involving a ladder, the sun, moon and stars, grapes and breadbaskets, fat and skinny cows, plump and skinny ears of grain, a statue, an enormous tree, a lion, bear, leopard and a mysterious ten-horned beast. In what seems like a "pizza dream," an unidentified Midianite soldier dreamed a loaf of barley bread rolled into their camp turning over their tents which was interpreted as a prediction of Gideon's military victory over them. No one ever said dreams weren't strange but we should value them because God seems to like communicating this way!

1. Why do you think God still uses dreams to communicate?

_____

_____

_____

_____

_____

_____

_____

_____

2. Does reading about the strange symbolism that God used to communicate in the Bible make your dreams seem "more normal"?

_____

_____

_____

_____

_____

_____

_____

3. What are some symbols from your dreams that rival some of the biblical dreams for unique symbolism (bring on the flying monkeys and singing radishes!)?

_____

_____

_____

_____

_____

_____

_____

How important are dreams to God? One-third of the Bible is devoted to dreams, visions and prophecy. "[The] Hebrew language makes little distinction between dreams and visions. Whether it was an angelic visitation, a dream, a vision, or other prophetic experience, it was all considered to be supernatural communication with God."[1] "We spend one-third of our lives asleep. By the time you're 60, you will have slept 20 years! Every night when you sleep, you dream"[2]—whether you remember it or not."

1. Do you usually remember your dreams when you wake in the morning? Have you ever tried to interpret them before?

_____

_____

_____

_____

_____

_____

_____

_____

_____

_____

_____

_____

2. Have you considered that God is trying to speak with you in your dreams?

_____

_____

_____

_____

_____

_____

_____

_____

3. Why would He want to do that?

_____

_____

_____

_____

_____

_____

_____

_____

A dream is a vehicle that God uses to convey His ideas, thoughts, and plans. It can be a parable incorporating components from daily life and culture to convey a concept you would not have thought of on your own. *Nothing deters His ability to get our attention.* God searches out every person, from the very youngest to the very oldest, from the nicest person to the not nice person. No one is too far away or hidden from His love. He uses a dream to go to anywhere on the planet to speak to even one person. In a dream, God can communicate to us in such a personalized way that no matter what belief system we are born into or have developed, we will be compelled to search for this One who knows and loves every tiny detail about us.

1. Write your response to this comment: "A dream is a message from eternity.[3]"

2. How would you explain God's communication through dreams to a friend who thinks dreams were only for the Bible, not now?

_____

_____

_____

_____

_____

_____

_____

_____

_____

_____

_____

_____

_____

_____

_____

_____

_____

_____

_____

Dreams are an amazing gift from a loving God, and the interpretation, wisdom, and strategy that He is delivering has our absolute best in mind.

> Trust in the Lord completely, and do not rely on your own opinions. With all your heart rely on him to guide you, and he will lead you in every decision you make. ...Don't think for a moment that you know it all, for wisdom comes when you adore him (Proverbs 3:5-7, TPT).

1. Does the thought of completely trusting God make you nervous? Why or why not?

_____

_____

_____

_____

_____

_____

_____

2. On a scale of 1-10 how convinced are you that God has your best in mind?

1 2 3 4 5 6 7 8 9 10

3. Have a conversation with Him now about this.

Dreams are an invitation to hear and partner with Heaven's wisdom. Jesus will go to whatever length necessary to build friendship with you. He has seen where you are and where you will be. He is waiting for an invitation to be on the journey with you so that He may equip you with wisdom and creativity to accomplish all you were made for. To Jesus, you are a history maker! He is looking forward, with much joy, to making this journey with you!

1. Do you believe that God wants a friendship or deeper relationship with you? Why or why not?

_____

_____

_____

_____

_____

_____

_____

_____

_____

_____

_____

_____

_____

_____

2. Write a prayer accepting Jesus's invitation to go on this journey with you.

_____

_____

_____

_____

_____

_____

_____

_____

_____

_____

_____

_____

_____

_____

_____

_____

_____

_____

_____

_____

As your body sleeps it's an opportunity for God to bypass your logical mind and your understanding. Since your spirit never sleeps, God has your full attention. He bypasses your logic for His. Then Jesus, the ultimate Storywriter, spins a tale that interweaves details from your life, including people you are familiar with into a fascinating storyline to captivate your imagination. The dream story may highlight an area of your life, help you solve a problem, or give you a different perspective on a decision you are about to make or a relationship you are currently in.

1. Write a synopsis of a dream which did one of the above. If you haven't had one of those experiences, see question 2.

2. Pick one of the three examples from above and write a prayer asking God to send you a dream about this specific circumstance.

_____

_____

_____

_____

_____

_____

_____

_____

_____

_____

_____

_____

_____

_____

_____

_____

_____

_____

God is the best teacher you can possibly want to learn from because He sees the big picture of your life—your past, present and future. A dream is an invitation to attend your own personal "God University." The subject of each class is you! Course development continues through your life with God's perspective of your circumstances—good and difficult, from conception to when you leave this life to join Him in Heaven. At the core of this study is God's very best plan for your life, focused with His perfect love. God is motivated to help you excel in His classroom.

1. Read and write a paraphrase of Jeremiah 29:11.

_____

_____

_____

_____

_____

_____

_____

_____

_____

_____

_____

_____

2. What would be the topic or title of the next class you would like to take at "God University"?

_____

_____

_____

_____

_____

_____

_____

_____

_____

_____

_____

_____

_____

_____

_____

_____

_____

_____

_____

A dream may be extremely personal. Our actions, thoughts, attitudes, and intentions are completely visible to God. He is not embarrassed of you, about you, or by you—ever! He is very pleased at how He made you. He knows when and where you need to mature so that your gifts are useful and you can accomplish all He has called you to. Be an excellent student. Stay humble; keep practicing hearing what God is saying. Stay close to His Word so you can learn all the wisdom you can without needing to retake the test.

1. Read Job 33:15-18. What are the three positive things about dreams mentioned in verses 16-17?

   a. _____

   _____

   _____

   b. _____

   _____

   _____

   c. _____

   _____

   _____

Sadly, most do not realize there is a very real game of thrones underway in the unseen eternal realm and that to defeat a spiritual foe you need spiritual weapons—the presence of God and knowledge of the gifts of the Spirit—to fulfill your destiny and shine like the stars forever.[4]

1. What spiritual weapons have you used to defeat the unseen realm?

_____

_____

_____

_____

_____

_____

_____

2. How can a dream from God be a spiritual weapon for you?

_____

_____

_____

_____

_____

_____

_____

Here is a list of some of the dreams we won't discuss in detail in this journal.

- Genesis 31:10-11—Jacob's Instructional Dream concerning the raising of goats

- Genesis 31:24—Laban's Dream

- Judges 7:13-15—Midianite Dream of the Barley Loaf

- 1 Kings 3:5-15—Solomon receives wisdom from God while in a dream.

- Daniel 5:12—Daniel Interprets the Handwriting on the Wall

- Matthew 1:20—Joseph's Dream to Take Mary as His Wife

- Matthew 2:12-13—The Wise Men's Dream of Warning

- Matthew 2:19—Joseph's Dream to Return to Israel

- Matthew 2:22—Joseph's Dream to move to Galilee

- Matthew 27:19—Pilate's Wife's Dream Concerning Jesus

1. Pick one of the dreams and look up the symbols and check a commentary.

2. Write what you learned about the dream and its meaning.

_____

_____

_____

_____

_____

_____

_____

_____

_____

_____

_____

_____

_____

_____

_____

_____

_____

_____

_____

You may be wondering, *Can I learn to interpret dreams?* Absolutely! God would not give dreams if He was not prepared to help us understand them.

1. How often have you had dreams you felt were from God?

_____

_____

_____

_____

_____

_____

_____

_____

2. How many nights per week do you usually dream?

_____

_____

_____

_____

_____

_____

_____

_____

3. Do you get multiple dreams or just one?

_____

_____

_____

_____

_____

_____

_____

_____

4. How well do you remember the dreams and details?

_____

_____

_____

_____

_____

_____

_____

_____

I SLEEP BUT MY HEART IS AWAKE

By far, the most important key to understanding dreams is the relationship you build with the One who gives dreams. The time you spend talking to Jesus, getting familiar with His Word, and simply understanding how He speaks is priceless. Make it your goal to understand your dreams from His eyes. When you take this step, He helps you gain His perspective of your life.

1. Read and write a paraphrase of James 4:8.

_____

_____

_____

_____

_____

_____

_____

_____

_____

_____

_____

_____

_____

2. List three ways you can build your relationship with God.

   a. _____

   _____

   _____

   b. _____

   _____

   _____

   c. _____

   _____

   _____

In order to interpret dreams you have to have the Holy Spirit's help. Dream interpretation is supernatural, not natural. The Holy Spirit holds the key. A dream that is difficult to understand is similar to a padlock. Only one key will open it. When Holy Spirit brings true revelation to a dream, it is like the key that aligns the tumblers of the lock and the lock pops open! The truth Holy Spirit reveals fills your heart with joy and purpose.

1. Read 1 Corinthians 2:7-12 in the NIV.

2. Who knows God's thoughts?

_____

_____

_____

_____

_____

_____

_____

3. Having the Spirit allows you to _____ .

"It is God's privilege to conceal things and the king's privilege to discover them" (Proverbs 25:2). At first glance this verse might seem discouraging but let's put it in different terms. If you ever hid Easter eggs, were you hiding them *from* your kids or were you hiding them *for* them? When God conceals a matter it's an invitation to pursue Him in a game of hide 'n seek.

1. Did you anticipate and experience great pleasure watching your kids search and find?

_____

_____

_____

_____

_____

_____

2. Jot down a pleasant Easter egg memory.

_____

_____

_____

_____

_____

_____

3. How does the Easter egg illustration apply to Proverbs 25:2?

_____

_____

_____

_____

_____

_____

_____

_____

_____

_____

_____

_____

_____

_____

_____

_____

_____

_____

_____

God created you to hear His voice. From the beginning His plan was that you would experience intimate relationship with Him.

Jesus wants to give you the genuine Holy Spirit. One line of His truth can change your life. The enemy may give information from his realm, but it's a cheap imitation of God's power-filled, accurate revelation. You are never too young or too old to learn to hear from the Holy Spirit.

Here are a few of the infinite ways Jesus communicates to us.

- Seeing (with my eyes)

- Hearing

- Smelling

- Tasting

- Sense or touch

- Dreams

- Daydreams

- Déjà vu

- Prophetic words from a trusted source

- Impressions

- Art and through pictures

- Numbers

- Colors

- Time (like seeing 4:44 on the clock)

- Calendar dates (Hebrew calendar or Gregorian calendar)

- Nature (see Romans 1:20)

- Animals or pets (see Genesis 30 and 41)

- Natural happenings around me

- My circumstances

- God's promises, His covenant (see Exodus 24)

- Bible, God's Word

- Visions (not quite asleep, but not awake)

- Open visions (like a mini-movie when awake)

There is no limit on Holy Spirit's forms of communication. God has given you His Word and authenticated it by laying His whole life down for you.

1. Circle the predominant ways that God speaks to you. Then thank Him for that.

2. What is the most surprising way God has spoken to you?

_____

_____

_____

_____

_____

_____

_____

3. Is there a place you've put God in a box and how have you done that?

_____

_____

_____

_____

_____

_____

_____

In our culture, science, psychology, or "enlightened thought" have been given the bulk of influence in defining the supernatural and its use. Our culture avoids considering the Creator's thoughts on the supernatural. Those who practice the counterfeit are readily accepted as relevant, ("always learning but never discover the revelation-knowledge of truth," 2 Timothy 3:7). The goal of this journal is to point you to the Trinity and scripture as the ultimate source of dream interpretation. Joseph said, "God is the only One who can explain the meaning of dreams" (Genesis 40:8, ICB). A key to understanding dreams is to recognize that all dreams and interpretation come from God and we must depend on His Spirit for interpretation.

1. The enemy has done a good job convincing people that dream interpretation should be relegated to the "new age crowd." How would you dispel this argument?

_____

_____

_____

_____

_____

_____

_____

2. How does 1 Timothy 6:20-21 relate to our current culture's opinion on the supernatural?

_____

_____

_____

_____

_____

_____

_____

_____

3. Do you agree with what Joseph said? Why or why not?

_____

_____

_____

_____

_____

_____

_____

_____

My prayer is that as you work through this journal God's true super-natural gifts and revelatory wisdom will increase, making simple what has seemed impossible or too difficult. We, as believers in God's Word, have access to answers—abundantly available—in the precious Word of God and the amazing Holy Spirit, who guides us into all truth.

1. Are you more likely to receive revelation from reading the Word or some other way?

2. How do you feel when you receive revelation or a word from God about your circumstance?

_____

_____

_____

_____

_____

_____

_____

_____

_____

_____

_____

"Never run to the world to learn how to grow in the things of the spirit. Run to the Word of God." [5]

John Paul Jackson[6]

The single best source for understanding dreams and dream inter-pretation—is the Bible. There is no other book that establishes godly wisdom, stabilizes your thoughts and actions, and comforts you in every situation and time of life.

All Scripture is given by inspiration of God, and is profitable for doctrine, for reproof, for correction, for instruction in righteousness, that the man of God may be complete, thoroughly equipped for every good work (2 Timothy 3:16-17).

1. What are four benefits that the Word of God provides according to Hebrews 4:12?

    a. _____

    _____

    b. _____

    _____

    c. _____

    _____

    d. _____

    _____

2. According to Hebrews 4:13 why can God give dreams that are relevant and specific for you?

_____

_____

_____

_____

_____

_____

_____

_____

_____

_____

_____

_____

_____

_____

_____

_____

_____

_____

The goal of interpretation is to catch the message of the dream to help the dreamer gain wisdom and work for positive change in his life. I will highlight five basic steps of dream interpretation:

The first basic step of dream interpretation is to write, records or draw the dream. You don't need to be concerned about grammar or punctuation. The main goal is to get all the details written. You may want to sketch; some dreams are best drawn or simply explained with lots of color or shapes. A digital voice recorder is effective particularly if you dream a song, tune, rhythm, or other sound. Whatever your recording device, keep it handy. Make sure you can turn it on when sleepy and speak the dream clearly so you don't miss details. Keep a written copy so that the dream is not lost if your device/recording becomes unavailable.

1. Will you use a pen and paper or a recording device?

    _____

2. Go put it there now!

    (You aren't allowed to proceed until you do step 2 above!) After writing or dictating the dream, ask Jesus for the interpretation. You may already understand what the dream is, or you may have no idea. Write what you have, always asking Holy Spirit for more understanding.

1. Why is it important to write or record the details of the dream?

_____

_____

_____

_____

_____

_____

_____

_____

_____

2. Do you have a hard time remembering dreams and their details?

_____

_____

_____

_____

_____

_____

_____

_____

_____

The second basic step of dream interpretation is to ask God to help you understand what the dream means.

1. Jot the synopsis of a recent dream.

_____

_____

_____

_____

_____

_____

_____

_____

_____

_____

_____

_____

_____

_____

_____

_____

_____

_____

_____

2. Write a prayer asking for help with interpretation and jot down
   the answer you receive.

_____

_____

_____

_____

_____

_____

_____

_____

_____

_____

_____

_____

_____

_____

_____

_____

_____

The third basic step of dream interpretation is to repeat the entire dream to yourself or to a friend. A trusted friend can be a key for understanding your dream. When you tell the dream to a friend, simply saying the dream out loud may help you understand it. When stumped by a dream, I call a friend, repeat the dream, and almost immediately understand what the dream is saying. Your friend may also have insight.

1. Who could you trust to share your dreams with?

    _____

    _____

    _____

    _____

2. Write down a day and a time this week that you will call/connect.

    _____

    _____

    _____

    _____

3. Set an alarm on your phone. (Seriously, do it now!)

The fourth basic step of dream interpretation is to define some of the metaphors in the dream. For instance, in a dream, money may represent what is valuable to the dreamer. What you spend money on is what you treasure (see Matthew 6:19-21). Eyes can represent vision or the ability to see in the spirit; a pair of glasses can represent your vision or the calling on your life; teeth may represent words. I have a certain pastor I respect and when he shows up in my dreams I know he represents the Lord. I'll include more on dream interpretation later.

1. Is there a certain person who represents someone else in your dreams? Who does he/she represent?

_____

_____

_____

_____

_____

_____

_____

_____

_____

_____

_____

_____

_____

2. List several metaphors you suspect might be significant in your dreams.

_____

_____

_____

_____

_____

_____

_____

_____

_____

_____

_____

_____

_____

_____

_____

_____

_____

_____

The fifth basic step of dream interpretation is to retell the dream story again with the various elements it contains and the understanding you've received. This can bring further clarification.

1. Do you now have a pen/paper or recording device on your nightstand? If not, you know what to do.

2. Which one of the five steps did you find most interesting and why?

_____

_____

_____

_____

_____

_____

_____

_____

_____

_____

_____

_____

_____

_____

Communication is never a problem with God. He understands not only your spoken language, He understands every single detail about your history, how you think, and why you process life as you do. He communicates by using a multitude of language tools. He will speak in words common to you by using pictures, numbers, colors, and stories that describe His thoughts. God uses word picture metaphors to take us to a higher place so we can understand His thoughts about us. I cannot know what Jesus is thinking unless I access God's Spirit.

1.   Read 1 Corinthians 2:14-16.

   a.   Who can't know the things of the Spirit?

   _____

   _____

   b.   Why can't he know spiritual things?

   _____

   _____

   c.   Who does know spiritual things?

   _____

   _____

   _____

Think about how priceless you are to God. He takes the time to "write" a script and then allows the parable or dream to play out on a stage in your mind while you sleep, all so you can "see" how He thinks about your life, learn His perspective, and receive guidance from Him.

A dream is like receiving an invitation to hear what God thinks of a current situation in your life. This is huge! The God of Heaven cares about even the simplest details of your life and will give you a scenario in your dreams that speaks about your thoughts, actions, plans, decisions, and relationships.

1. What area of your life most needs guidance or direction?

_____

_____

_____

_____

_____

_____

_____

_____

_____

_____

_____

2. Write a prayer asking God to answer your request.

_____

_____

_____

_____

_____

_____

_____

_____

_____

_____

_____

_____

_____

"Head knowledge is what you learned,
spirit knowledge is what the Spirit of God
is telling you about the dream."

John Paul Jackson[7]

Our dreams are mostly symbolic. They are often ignored because on the surface they don't make any sense. God speaks in a figurative language we frequently don't understand. These confusing symbols do not make the dream invalid or untrue. We just need to dig out the hidden meaning in God's dream language. God loves to use every form of literary tool to stretch us and get us to pursue Him for answers. No code, language, formula or system is unknown or hidden from Him. God speaks in story or parable language, a riddle, or an enigma so that the dreamer will pursue the interpretation and ultimately find, build, and strengthen the relationship with Him.

1. Look up and write down the most relevant definition of the following ways that God can speak:

   a. A parable –

   _____

   _____

   b. A riddle –

   _____

   _____

   c. An enigma -

   _____

   _____

Go online and look up the free, Biblical Dream Dictionary (http://www.unlockingyourdreams.org/dream-dictionary/) or find a reputable dream dictionary compiled by reputable people.

1. Spend some time looking at the different symbols and their interpretations.

2. Jot down images that show up most frequently in your dreams and write their potential meaning.

_____

_____

_____

_____

_____

_____

"Knowledge of biblical symbols is like identifying the edges of a jigsaw puzzle. They set the parameters of the puzzle; The Holy Spirit fills in the rest of the puzzle." [8]

According to John Paul Jackson there are three biblical types of dreams.[9] The Simple Message Dream is obvious and requires no need for interpretation. In Matthew 2:13 Joseph understood the dream. "When they had gone, an angel of the Lord appeared to Joseph in a dream. 'Get up,' he said, 'take the child and his mother and escape to Egypt. Stay there until I tell you, for Herod is going to search for the child to kill him.'" The next dream is a Simple Symbolic Dream. God uses metaphors and imagery to speak to us. Joseph's dream, Genesis 37:9-10, had only the moon and stars and everyone understood it to the point they wanted to kill him. These dreams might be full of symbols but they are easily understood. Next is the Complex Symbolic Dream which require revelation knowledge or possibly someone who has a gift of interpreting dreams. Nebuchadnezzar's dream in Daniel 2 is an example that required divine revelation to interpret. "Surely your God is the God of gods and the Lord of kings and a revealer of mysteries, for you were able to reveal this mystery" (Daniel 2:47).

In the beginning you might feel that your Simple Symbolic Dreams are Complex Symbolic Dreams because they seem so hard to inter-pret, but with time and practice interpretation will become easier.

1. Have you ever had a dream that you immediately understood the interpretation of?

   _____

   _____

   _____

   _____

2. What was it about?

_____

_____

_____

_____

_____

_____

_____

_____

_____

_____

_____

_____

_____

_____

_____

_____

_____

_____

_____

_____

_____

_____

3. What was the theme of your last complex dream?

_____

_____

_____

_____

_____

_____

_____

_____

_____

_____

_____

_____

_____

_____

_____

_____

_____

_____

A dream is a parable given in your sleep. Parables were Jesus's favorite teaching tool whenever He taught on earth. It seems that word pictures or metaphors are Jesus's favorite tool to help you understand His thoughts. Word pictures cross language, culture, thought, and religious barriers, and they can give us a common language with God.

We use the term *metaphor* to identify something we recognize from our own life and bring a spiritual meaning or lesson to. For example: An entrance ramp is the way our motor vehicles get onto the highway. Used as a metaphor, we understand this "High-way" is the higher way of understanding and accessing the Spirit of God. You may also see this represented as a *high* school or a place of *higher* learning.

The disciples would ask, "What are You talking about, Jesus?" because they were trying to grasp His thoughts with their natural minds without accessing the Spirit of God.

1. Since you've started interpreting your dreams can you relate to the disciples' frustration?

    _____

    _____

    _____

    _____

2. What was Jesus's response to them in Matthew 13:11-12?

_____

_____

_____

_____

_____

_____

_____

_____

3. Compose a prayer asking for eyes to see and ears to hear.

_____

_____

_____

_____

_____

_____

_____

_____

_____

Jesus can speak to us about any subject known to man and those not yet understood—with astonishing detail. It is fun to learn His language and wisdom and to realize His message is specifically for us. For instance, an airline pilot may dream the exact specifications of an airplane engine, specific mechanical information, airports, wind speeds, or other information related to flying. Because this is his profession and/or hobby, he will better understand what God is saying in the dream. It is similar to having a secret code between you and Jesus.

1. Read and write a paraphrase of Jeremiah 1:5.

_____

_____

_____

_____

2. What common or well-understood symbols might God use to communicate with you?

_____

_____

_____

_____

It can be tempting to rest on one interpretation or definition for a metaphor. Guard against this and be ready to hear God's creative and unique thoughts about you.

Meanings may change because of the context of the dream. For instance, in one dream a lion may represent Jesus, and in another dream a lion may be seeking to devour you (1 Peter 5:8). The context of the dream is vital!

As you mature, your perspective changes and metaphors can begin to represent different things. Dream interpretation is fun because you'll soon realize that you have a unique language that is just between you and Jesus.

1. Have you ever had or given a nickname or purposely mispronounced words to make them funny? Write a few down:

_____

_____

_____

_____

_____

_____

_____

_____

_____

_____

2. Name some biblical images with double meanings (Matthew 13:33, 1 Corinthians 5:6-8).

_____

_____

_____

_____

_____

_____

_____

_____

_____

_____

_____

_____

Spiritual dreams were valued as a divine encounter with God. Jewish bedtime customs include inviting God to come and speak to them through dreams.[10]

Joseph was a dreamer from a young age. He was 17 when he had two significant dreams. Joseph was the second-youngest member of his family and his father's favorite.

Listen to this dream I had. We were all out in the field gathering bundles of wheat. All of a sudden my bundle stood straight up and your bundles circled around it and bowed down to mine (Genesis 37:6-7).

1. According to Genesis 37:5-8 what was his brothers' response when Joseph told the first dream to them?

2. Why do you think all his brothers immediately knew the meaning of the dream?

Joseph must have been a prolific dreamer. Genesis 37:9-11 records how he told his family his second dream. (You would think he would have learned the first time!) This is probably indicative of a pride issue that God had to painfully remove from him over a period of years.

1. Read Genesis 37:9-11.

    How did Joseph's brothers respond to the second dream?

    _____

    _____

    _____

    _____

    _____

    _____

    _____

2. What were the two things verse 11 says his father did?

    _____

    _____

    _____

    _____

    _____

    _____

    _____

Regardless of how Joseph was treated and the difficulty he endured, Joseph learned to place his confidence in God. Most of his life was directed by dreams. Instead of running from God or blaming God for his difficult circumstances, Joseph learned how God was speaking to him and chose to gain wisdom from his dreams. His relationship with God grew deeper and his dream-interpretation skills were profound. Joseph was able to bless those around him through his skills. Read Genesis 40:1-23.

1. Why were the cupbearer and the baker sad? (verses 6-8)

_____

_____

_____

_____

_____

_____

2. What would the end result be for the cupbearer and the baker according to Joseph's interpretation of their dreams?

_____

_____

_____

_____

_____

_____

3. Did it happen the way Joseph predicted? (verses 20-22)

_____

_____

_____

_____

_____

_____

_____

_____

_____

_____

_____

_____

_____

_____

_____

_____

_____

_____

_____

Eventually, Joseph's two childhood dreams came true and were vital to the rescue of Joseph's whole family (whose descendants would become the nation of Israel). The dreams were key to Joseph's success. The wisdom he had attained from his relationship with God gave him the ability to sustain the entire nation of Egypt through deadly famine (see Genesis 37, 39–50).

1. How could a dream keep you from losing hope in difficult circumstances?

2. Read Genesis 41:1-57. Why did God give Pharaoh the same dream in two forms?

_____

_____

_____

_____

_____

_____

_____

_____

_____

_____

_____

_____

_____

_____

_____

_____

_____

_____

Like Joseph, you are designed to impact the earth. You were not placed here by accident or happenstance; rather, God has allowed you to be born into the right place and time. You were made in the likeness of God and created with an aspect of God's nature that no one else can duplicate or operate in. You carry tremendous potential.

1. Write your emotional response to the following: "When God created you, He created a dream and wrapped a body around that dream to fulfill it." —Lou Engle[11]

_____

_____

_____

_____

_____

_____

_____

_____

_____

_____

_____

_____

_____

_____

2. Write a response back to God.

_____
_____
_____
_____
_____
_____
_____
_____
_____
_____
_____
_____
_____
_____
_____
_____
_____
_____
_____
_____

Every motion picture or play has a script, complete with characters and personality traits that help bring a story to life. When you have a dream, you've just heard from the brilliant Scriptwriter and Director of your life and you have permission to ask for clarification of His thoughts. God will reveal information in a dream or vision that you could not possibly know in the natural. He sees the big picture and is giving you access to the script.

1. What kind of script is your life following: drama, comedy, tragedy, action, thriller, horror, etc.?

_____

_____

_____

_____

2. How do you feel about your life's script?

_____

_____

_____

_____

_____

_____

_____

_____

3. How would you like to rewrite it?

_____

_____

_____

_____

_____

_____

_____

_____

_____

_____

_____

_____

_____

_____

_____

_____

_____

_____

_____

_____

Do you have to believe in God to get a dream from Him? No, it does not matter if the dreamer is a believer. Everyone has the ability to receive dreams from God. From ancient times to the present we have stories from people of all age groups, professions, and belief systems not only dreaming, but giving credit to God for their dreams.

1. Read Genesis 20:1-6, Genesis 41:1-8, Daniel 2:1-49, Daniel 4:1-37. Jot down these unbelieving kings. Why do you think God gave them dreams?

_____

_____

_____

_____

_____

_____

_____

_____

_____

_____

_____

_____

_____

_____

2. According to Matthew 5:45, why would God send a dream to an unbeliever?

_____

_____

_____

_____

_____

_____

_____

3. Who is an unbeliever you will commit to pray for to receive dreams from the Lord?

_____

_____

_____

_____

_____

_____

_____

Have you ever awakened to realize the memory of your dream is quickly slipping away? Dreams are quickly lost. Memories fade, perceptions of the dream can change, and details can be forgotten. It is very difficult to recover a dream once it is lost. Ask God to help you remember then spend some time worshipping. A situation later in the day may trigger the memory of what you dreamed. If not, pray that the dream will be repeated.

1. As a general rule do you remember your dreams when you wake up?

_____

_____

_____

_____

_____

_____

2. Do they come back to you later in the day?

_____

_____

_____

_____

_____

_____

Before you get out of bed ask the Lord if you had any dreams. Try to recall one or two of the details. Often your memory will kick in and the rest of the dream will come. It is important to write your dreams down. Whether you have dreamed for a long time or are new to this, it takes effort to get into the habit of documenting the dream as soon as you receive it. When we ask God to speak to us, it is important to journal the dreams He gives us. This builds honor in our heart toward God. When we honor what God has given we open up the possibility of receiving more. Here are journaling tips from John Paul Jackson's *Unlocking Dreams – Student Manual:*[12]

1. Date your dream at the top of your page and note where you were at when you received it.

2. Record your dream, including as much detail as you remember.

3. Write out possible interpretations underneath that.

4. Write out questions about the dream. "Why was the car green?" "Why was my mother in that dream?" etc.

5. Title your dream—Boil your dream down to its simplest form. Always let your title reflect the simplest meaning of the dream. Oftentimes, you will have the interpretation of your dream just by determining a fitting title.

Always be listening. You are never too young or too old for Jesus to speak to you. Keep the journal and a pen beside your bed. Write the dream as soon as possible. If you are awakened by a dream, even in the middle of the night, that is the time to write it down. It is risky to tell yourself "I'll write it down in the morning." Dreams are quickly lost and when you wake you may have already forgotten. Recording your dreams takes some discipline, but you will be rewarded by the practice.

1. Do you have the notebook and pen by your bed?

Yes   No

2. If not, go now and rectify this tragic situation. (Seriously, what are you waiting for?)

3. How regularly are you recording your dreams?

_____

_____

_____

_____

_____

_____

_____

_____

When you write down dreams, it makes it possible to review what you were shown over long periods of time. This dream history builds understanding for interpretation. It is fun to find patterns, repeating stories, or scenarios in your dreams, and it gives understanding to your personal dream language.

1. If you have previously written a dream in another journal, find and read it. Write the synopsis here:

_____

_____

_____

_____

_____

_____

_____

_____

_____

_____

_____

_____

_____

_____

_____

_____

2. Do you have more insight to the dream now? If so, what?

_____

_____

_____

_____

_____

_____

_____

_____

_____

_____

_____

_____

_____

_____

_____

_____

_____

I SLEEP BUT MY HEART IS AWAKE

When journaling a dream, it is important to write what you literally saw in the dream, but when interpreting, it is important to look at the dream through Jesus's eyes and understand His thoughts. Not all of what you find in your research may apply to the dream's interpretation, but the search for what Jesus may be saying is captivating and fun. I've learned to be content knowing that God's thoughts and ways are far above ours.

1. Read and write a paraphrase of Isaiah 55:8-9.

_____

_____

_____

_____

2. Have you looked up some symbols from your dreams in the dream dictionary?

Yes   No

3. What is the most interesting one you found and what does it mean to you?

_____

_____

_____

_____

When you have a dream, the first assumption you can make is "because I dreamed it, it is about me." Most of your dreams are about your own circumstances, people you know, and things familiar to you.

There will most likely be other people in your dream. Who else has consistently showed up? The question to ponder is, *What does this person mean to me?* What do they represent? Think about the role the person plays and how their position or occupation applies to the dream. Examples: a parent may be a guardian or leader. A pastor may be Jesus or a shepherd. A favorite teacher may be Holy Spirit or one who gives knowledge/wisdom. A doctor may be one bringing physical or spiritual healing.

1. Write a synopsis of a recent dream.

_____

_____

_____

_____

_____

_____

_____

_____

_____

_____

_____

2. What is *your role* in the dream? Are you the main character, or are you simply observing?

_____

_____

_____

_____

_____

_____

_____

3. Who else is in the dream? What do they represent?

_____

_____

_____

_____

_____

_____

_____

What are you doing in the dream—are you working? At school, learning? What activity are you involved in? Are you in motion, such as flying or running? Are you using some form of transportation like a bicycle, airplane or bus? These may represent your life's calling, a trade, or business. Vehicles may represent a ministry you are in or called to. Be sure to write down what catches your attention or what is highlighted, as it is important for interpretation. Jesus is speaking, using your interests to highlight His thoughts about you.

1. What were you riding the last time you were on a vehicle in your dream?

_____

_____

_____

_____

2. What does that represent?

_____

_____

_____

_____

Where the dream takes place is significant. Each location can have a significant meaning and its own important role in interpretation. Take note of the size and the purpose of the building.

A house may represent a ministry, a church, a personal life situation, your life or family. A school or classroom could represent a training period, a place of teaching or a ministry with teaching anointing.

1. Answer the following questions about several recent dreams:

   a. What is the location—a town, city, country, building, park?

   _____

   b. Are you in your home or someone else's?

   _____

   c. Are you in a specific part of your house—bathroom, kitchen, upstairs, basement, bedroom, garage?

   _____

   d. Is this place familiar?

   _____

   e. Is there a body of water, swimming pool, river, lake, ocean, etc.?

   _____

2. Using the dream dictionary, write down some of the symbolism, what it means and what you think God is trying to communicate through it:

_____

_____

_____

_____

_____

_____

_____

_____

_____

_____

_____

_____

_____

_____

_____

_____

_____

_____

_____

How do you feel in the dream? How you wake up feeling during and after the dream is also important. Emotions like happiness, sadness, anger, fear, disgust, confidence, peace, and boldness all show up in dreams and are important to note. Try to identify where you feel this emotion in your daily life. This might be the area of your waking life that God is speaking about.

It is also important that you record the intensity of the emotion. For example, "In my dream, the lion was roaring very loud, then he turned and roared right in my face! I woke, and my heart was pounding!"

You may also feel emotions that seem out of place: "Although the lion was terrifying, I was not afraid and actually felt boldness."

You may have discernment of good or evil from how you feel in a dream. Snakes or skunks may be a signal of something evil. A bright sunny day, a playful puppy, or a smiling person may be a signal of something very good.

Jesus is the happiest person you'll ever meet. Sometimes He or an angel will appear in your dream as a very happy person. If He appears as a lion, you'll know He is good and not going to harm you.

1. Jot down a very emotional situation from a dream.

_____

_____

_____

_____

_____

2. List a time an emotion seemed out of place.

_____

_____

_____

_____

_____

_____

_____

_____

_____

_____

"Repetitious Dreams can be given by God to bring added clarity to a matter. Remember, the more clearly God speaks on a matter, the more accountable you are to obey what He has spoken." [13]

John Paul Jackson

When seeking to interpret a dream and something is repeated, pay close attention because it is God highlighting something important. When God repeats something, it's a sign the dream is important or the topic is urgent. The dream comes to remind you that you were not listening the first time. If you are experiencing repeated dreams, you need to take note because God wants you to act. The more you keep record of your dreams, the more you'll begin to recognize the repeated elements.

1. Jot the synopsis of any repeating dreams or repeating symbols in your dreams.

_____

_____

_____

_____

_____

_____

_____

_____

_____

_____

_____

_____

_____

_____

2. Have you had a series of two or three dreams that all seem connected? What was the common element?

_____

_____

_____

_____

_____

_____

_____

_____

_____

_____

_____

_____

_____

_____

_____

_____

_____

Details are important in dream interpretation. Write down the date and the exact time you dreamed it, if you know. If you don't know the exact time, write something like "before midnight," "after midnight," or "around 4:00 a.m." Whatever stands out, is highlighted, or is impressed in your memory, is worth writing down.

1. Answer these questions for a recent dream:

    a. Color or black and white?

    _____

    b. Numbers?

    _____

    c. Is the dream dark or light?

    _____

    d. What was the main story in the dream?

    _____

    e. How did you feel in the dream?

    _____

It is also possible that the dream may actually come true. An event may happen soon after you have the dream and you'll realize this event is what the dream was about.

Remember: If the interpretation connects to your understanding of the dream or is confirmed in your heart, you've correctly interpreted the dream. The interpretation usually brings a confident feeling of understanding. If you have any hesitation that you have the interpretation correct, wait until you learn more.

1. Jot the synopsis of a dream that you feel confident you interpreted correctly.

_____

_____

_____

_____

_____

_____

_____

_____

_____

_____

_____

_____

_____

2. Have you ever had a dream that came true? Did it surprise you? Jot it down.

_____

_____

_____

_____

_____

_____

_____

_____

_____

_____

_____

_____

_____

_____

_____

_____

_____

Here are a few practical tips: Develop a bedtime routine that focuses on the Lord. Don't go to bed right after watching TV. As you wind down, or even while in bed, read your Bible, listen to worship music or a good teaching. Dedicate times of sleep to the Lord and ask for good sleep. Ask God to speak to you in dreams and help you to remember them. Talk to Him as you fall asleep, telling Him how important your dreams are to you and that you want to remember your dreams and write them down. Thank Jesus in advance for any dreams He wants to give you. If possible wake up naturally or set your alarm to something that is quiet or melodious. Get rid of the heart-pounding, knee-jerking, blaring alarm.

1. What emotional state are you in when your head hits the pillow? Contemplative, stressed, etc. What changes do you need to make?

    _____

    _____

    _____

2. The above paragraph has many suggestions. How many have you implemented? How will you make the others a habit?

    _____

    _____

    _____

3. Ask the Lord to help you develop a prayer life as you go to sleep and when you wake during the night.

Jesus is always talking. He has great things to say and He wants to talk to you, about you. He is not giving you a story at night simply for your entertainment. He has something important to speak into your life. But, it takes an investment of time to become good at anything—an instrument, sports, etc. Dream interpretation is no different. Don't give up if understanding dreams is difficult at first, learning to interpret your dreams takes practice, time, and relationship with God. Remember, you are in the process of becoming an excellent interpreter of dreams. This is a lifelong practice. If you are willing to dive into the learning process, the return on this investment is well worth the cost.

1. Based on how often you write your dreams and pray over them, how seriously are you taking this form of communication with God?

_____

_____

_____

_____

_____

_____

_____

_____

2. Ask Him to help you do a better job of connecting with His heart through dreams.

A dream is like a parable or a short story with details that are familiar to you. It is intended to captivate your attention and curiosity. God is inviting you to pursue Him. He wants you to engage in the dream story that will help you see what is in your own heart. When you search out the correct interpretation, you will get a clearer perspective of your own heart without relying on your own reasoning, logic, or intellect. In other words, when I try to consider a problem in my life, I may come to my own conclusions instead of hearing God's wisdom on the subject. Dreams break through the barriers so that we can hear God's answer.

1. Read and write a paraphrase of Psalm 16:7.

_____

_____

_____

_____

2. I came to my own conclusion instead of God's the time I...

_____ .

_____

What if I don't dream?" "I never dream." "I do not remember my dreams." "God does not speak to me in dreams." These statements are examples of "negative agreements" or "negative declarations" that you should never say. Scientists have proven that everyone dreams every night but some people just don't remember. Sleep studies read people's brain waves using electrodes. When we will fall asleep, our brain is in an alpha state, then the brain moves to the lower theta waves and finally to delta, the lowest wave. Then we cycle back to alpha and start dreaming. Every time we return to alpha, the amount of dream time increases. In eight hours of sleep, the last hour is going to be almost all dream time.

Ask Jesus to help you dream and remember your dreams. When you wake, journal everything you remember or what you are thinking about when you wake. You may be surprised to find that you just were not paying attention to or recalling your dreams. It may take practice to begin remembering your dreams.

1. Search your heart. Ask God to forgive you for rejecting His methods of communication.

2. Read and write a paraphrase of James 4:2. Then ask God to help you remember your dreams.

_____

_____

_____

_____

3. If you still don't have a way to record your dreams by your bed, do this now! This indicates you don't believe you'll get dreams or you don't care enough to do anything with them.

If you or someone you trusted in the past attributed your dreams to the enemy, ask God to teach you to hear from Him by whatever method He chooses to use. From this time on, ask Jesus what He wants to say to you, listen to His voice, and refuse to give credit to any other source.

1. Write some of the ways God has communicated with you.

   _____

   _____

   _____

   _____

2. Write a prayer inviting God to communicate with you in a way He previously has not.

   _____

   _____

   _____

   _____

   _____

   _____

   _____

   _____

Sin can block our dreams. When we refuse to forgive others, it *will block our communication with God* (see Mark 11:25). Forgive others and walk in love. Forgiveness allows healing to begin in our heart, thus opening our ability to hear from God.

Wrong choices we make directly affect our ability to hear from God. Run to Jesus and into His love. Ask Him to restart your ability to hear from Him. Also read Exodus 20:3-17. Finally, have a thankful heart, regardless of whether you remember your dreams or not.

1. Pray this sample prayer or write your own:

    I'm so thankful for You, Jesus. I know You are thinking good thoughts about me all the time. If You choose to give me a dream, I am blessed. If You choose to be silent as I sleep, I am blessed. I love how You speak to me and how You created me with the ability to hear Your thoughts. Your willingness to give me wisdom, knowledge, and revelation makes my heart strong and keeps me from fear and doubt. Turn my pillow into a ladder, like You did for Jacob; may I see Your glory when I sleep. Thank You for including me in Your dreams. I dedicate this time of sleep to You. Thank You, Jesus, for who You are and for how You love and take such good care of me.

_____

_____

_____

_____

_____

_____

_____

_____

_____

_____

_____

_____

_____

_____

_____

_____

_____

_____

_____

2. Read Genesis 28:11-12. Think about this passage the rest of the day. This is called meditating on God's Word as mentioned in Psalm 1:2, 119:97, and Joshua 1:8.

Dreaming is good and necessary for your brain like food and water are necessary for your body. Your body must have sleep so that your brain, organs, and heart will continue to work properly. When you lack good sleep, you may feel more stressed, frustrated, or sad. Good sleep helps you feel hopeful and happy and brings motivation to accomplish projects. Dreams are equally important to your emotional health. This nightly brain refresh even boosts your ability to fight off sickness or to recover from injury. In order to get these benefits you must sleep.

1.   How many hours per night do you sleep?

_____

2.   What percentage of the time do you wake feeling refreshed?

_____

_____

3.   Ask the Lord for a strategy to help you sleep better.

_____

_____

_____

_____

_____

_____

_____

Dreams may trigger all sorts of reactions—laughter, tears, embarrassment, outrage, or even revulsion. Typically, these odd dreams are written off as "pizza dreams." However, because you witnessed an impossible situation in the dream, you may stumble onto an excellent bit of wisdom that will apply to your life.

Pizza dreams can be valuable. They may seem impossible to interpret, but ask Holy Spirit and search out the meaning of every dream you are blessed to receive. Remember, an embarrassing, offensive, impossible, or crazy storyline in a pizza dream may be the key to helping you remember the dream.

1. Revisit the first question in the book (currently page 12) and re-read the symbolism God used to communicate in the Bible. Does it make you feel better about your dreams?

2. Write a synopsis of the craziest pizza dream you can remember.

_____

_____

_____

_____

_____

_____

_____

_____

_____

_____

_____

_____

_____

_____

_____

_____

_____

_____

_____

_____

_____

3. What are several symbols that show up in your dreams that you
    think might have legitimate meaning?

_____

_____

_____

_____

_____

_____

_____

_____

Sometimes our dreams are emotionally charged. Jesus never gives us a *spirit* of fear, but He allows our human emotions to alert us to this present danger threatening our spiritual and physical life. Physical reactions like breathing hard, sweating, or suddenly waking are a part of the normal adrenaline rush you get when in danger.

"When I first woke from this dream, I thought it was a nightmare! I was completely covered with sweat, shaking, and wondering if this was going to happen to me in reality. I could have discarded the dream, thinking the enemy was involved in some way. But, I wrote down the dream and did not go back to it until after enough time had passed that I was no longer emotionally stirred. Had I interpreted the dream immediately, the emotion attached to it may have skewed the interpretation negatively."

It is wise put an emotionally stirring dream's interpretation on hold for several hours, a full day, or longer if the dream is highly emotional. Try repeating the dream to friends so the dream will become clearer and less tied to emotion.

1. Write a synopsis of an emotionally charged dream you've had:

_____

_____

_____

_____

_____

_____

_____

_____

_____

_____

_____

_____

_____

2. Were you able to eventually interpret it? Was the interpretation encouraging, discouraging, a warning, etc.?

_____

_____

_____

_____

3. What was the main message the Lord was trying to communicate?

_____

_____

_____

_____

_____

_____

_____

_____

Always write down what you feel in the dream. We were created to experience life. God made our minds and bodies able to feel joy, sadness, and fear as a way to process what is happening around us. In our dreams, we can experience emotion just like when we are awake. When writing the dream, be careful to not interpret the dream as you write it down. Intense feelings can lead you to add something to the dream that is not there.

After you've journaled the dream, put it away. Intense emotion makes your heart vulnerable and can easily lead you into a negative mindset.

1. Read and write a paraphrase of 2 Timothy 1:7.

   _____

   _____

   _____

   _____

2. Write a prayer asking God for His thoughts and interpretations to come to you at the right time.

   _____

   _____

   _____

   _____

   _____

   _____

We want to interpret our dreams with a *sound mind* and with God's heart as our guide. God has the absolute best plans for you and is planning your future. He is trying to bring encouragement and spur you on to accomplish greater things than you can imagine. He is the ultimate life coach.

1. Read and paraphrase Jeremiah 29:11.

_____

_____

_____

_____

_____

_____

_____

2. Read and paraphrase Psalm 27:13.

_____

_____

_____

_____

_____

_____

_____

110   I SLEEP BUT MY HEART IS AWAKE

You might wonder, *Now what do I do with this revelation?* After correctly interpreting a dream, then comes the application, which is just as important. Ask the Holy Spirit for direction.

1. Does the revelation you received require a change, action, or a special prayer focus, etc.?

    _____

    _____

2. What is your strategy for implementing this change?

    _____

    _____

    _____

    _____

    _____

    _____

    _____

    _____

    _____

    _____

3. Pray and ask the Lord for His help implementing the change and be sure to thank Him for communicating with you about it!

Dreams offer the dreamer the opportunity to change. A dream can teach us to pray in agreement with Jesus about what is on His heart. When we dream something that is difficult or makes us angry, in that moment, we are called to agree with Heaven and ask for change according to God's Word. We ask for God's thoughts and His plan for change. Be one who will say "yes" and agree with what is on Jesus's heart.

A dream may give you a prayer assignment from Jesus. To be really effective in prayer, listen to what Jesus has on His mind. He is always looking for people to pray in agreement with Heaven for God's Kingdom plan and ideas to be established here on earth.

When we wake from a dream, there is no pressure to think up great-sounding, lofty prayers. We can simply agree with the Father as He accomplishes His word. When we join in with the great 24/7 prayer meeting in Heaven, we are joining with the prayer that Jesus prayed to His Father, "Your kingdom come. Your will be done on earth as it is in heaven" (Matthew 6:10, NKJV). Here is an example of how you can pray when you wake from an intercession dream:

> Jesus, this dream frustrated me, scared me, made me angry (etc., tell Him how you feel). I know You want to bring change, and I agree with Your plan. I ask that You will open the eyes and ears of those who do not know they are in a trap. I ask You to give a way of escape to those who are captivated by lies. I agree with You, Your Kingdom come, Your will be done on earth as it is in Heaven. In Jesus's Name. Amen.

1. Read and write a paraphrase of Ezekiel 22:30 and tell the Lord that you are volunteering:

_____

_____

_____

_____

2. Write your prayer to volunteer:

_____

_____

_____

_____

_____

_____

_____

_____

_____

_____

_____

_____

_____

When a dream is dark or has an uneasy feeling, you might think that the enemy is speaking. However, you should never go to the enemy for interpretation. John 8:42-44 states that the enemy is a liar. The Bible makes it very clear that all true dream interpretation belongs to God.

1. Read and write a paraphrase of Genesis 40:8.

2. Read and write a paraphrase of Daniel 2:26-28.

Does the enemy want you to know his plans against you? No. Does Jesus want you to see the enemy's plans? Yes! He knows what is in darkness, and He exposes it! (See Daniel 2:22.) Jesus works for our success and will always *expose the enemy's plans* against us, revealing the *strategy* to defeat him. God does not give us a spirit of fear, but He may allow us to experience the fear the enemy's plan will produce. God wants to give you the confidence needed to defeat the enemy.

1. Do most of your dreams seem light and bright or have a negative, dark feeling to them?

_____

_____

_____

_____

_____

2. Which of the enemy's plans has the Lord exposed to you in a dream?

_____

_____

_____

_____

_____

_____

What is the purpose of a nightmare? Remember: The One who is interested in destroying the works of the enemy and exposing his plans is God! Many nightmares are overwhelming but are merciful warnings from God to keep the dreamer from trouble, expose a trap or offer a path of escape from trouble. A true friend will lovingly tell the truth to keep you from a negative experience. Jesus is the best friend you'll ever have.

Of the hundreds of scary dreams we've heard, it is hard to identify a single dream created by the enemy. Rather, the dream has been given so that the enemy's evil plan will be fully exposed. The enemy's plans are scary. Uncovering his evil is not fun to see. A scary dream is allowed so that you may tap into God's brilliant strategy to defeat and fully destroy the works of the enemy in your life. We have God's Word and His authority to shut the spiritual door and stop the enemy from entering.

1. Write a synopsis of a scary dream you have had.

_____

_____

_____

_____

_____

_____

_____

_____

_____

_____

2. Ask if this dream is from Him. Is it a warning?

3. Ask for insight. What could this dream mean?

Dreams of dying are not normally about the person seen in the dream in a literal sense, but are symbolic about something that is passing away or departing from your life. The type of death may be important to note. Watch, though, to see if resurrection is on the other side.

You may feel like the enemy is trying to terrify you in a dream, when actually God is exposing a problem that resides in your home or community, and this has stirred Him to come to your defense. He may be showing Himself available to intervene. It is important to consider these questions when looking at your dreams.

1. Is God exposing something that you need to know so that you can avoid trouble and stop the enemy?

    _____

    _____

    _____

    _____

2. Am I giving the enemy an open door or gate into my life? What is it?

    _____

    _____

    _____

    _____

When a dream has dark elements like a dark sky, a dark room, or is in black and white, Jesus wants to bring an issue to your attention so you can deal with it. If you wake up with an adrenaline rush or in panic mode, refuse to agree with the spirit of fear; instead, agree with the Spirit of love, power, and sound mind (2 Timothy 1:7).

Next, talk to Jesus. Typically you'll know exactly what sin you've participated with that brought on this dream or experience. Don't disregard the prompting that is in your own heart. Simply tell Jesus everything and ask for His solution. Look for God's strategy in the dream to defeat the enemy.

The way you counsel and correct me makes me praise you more, for your whispers in the night give me wisdom, showing me what to do next (Psalm 16:7).

Instead of immediately assuming the enemy is speaking in the dream, focus on what Jesus is revealing.

1. Ask God to show you how the enemy gained access to your life. Write your answer.

    _____

    _____

    _____

2. Pray over yourself—ask God for His forgiveness for whatever action opened a door to the enemy and then declare scripture over your life. God's Word is a powerful weapon against the enemy. Continue to meditate on the scripture throughout the day.

Transitioning from this life to our heavenly home is a natural part of life but we don't want it to happen outside of God's timing. If you have a dream involving your death, it is a good practice to immediately bring the dream to Jesus and declare His Word.

1. Paraphrase Psalm 118:17 and turn it into a prayer.

_____

_____

_____

_____

_____

_____

_____

_____

_____

_____

_____

_____

_____

_____

_____

_____

2. Do you have fears or worries that might be coming out in your dreams? What are they?

_____

_____

_____

_____

_____

_____

_____

_____

_____

_____

_____

_____

_____

_____

_____

_____

_____

_____

A death dream may alert us to a loved one's impending death. This may be a compassionate opportunity to say what we must say to our loved one with whatever time we have left. These dream experiences can begin to prepare us for future loss so that we will not despair but have confidence that God knows the number of everyone's days. Jesus is available to give us abundant hope and the comfort of Heaven.

1. Look up the name of the person who died in your dream in a name dictionary. (Their name's meaning may be the key to understanding the interpretation.) Write the information you find.

_____

_____

_____

_____

2. Run to Jesus; ask Him what you should do when confronted with a specific death dream! Write the answer.

_____

_____

_____

_____

When we experience death in a dream, it prompts us to recognize the seriousness of the moment. God is alerting us to speak His life into the situation, agree with His strategy, and have confidence that this person's life and salvation is in Jesus's hands.

1. Who is a person you need to begin praying for consistently?

_____

2. Write a prayer on their behalf:

_____

_____

_____

_____

_____

_____

_____

_____

_____

_____

_____

_____

When a dream involves death, it is easy to automatically believe the worst-case scenario—a friend or family member is going to die. I want to encourage you—*do not jump to this conclusion about a death dream.*

A dream may not be speaking of physical death but rather an issue that needs to "die," a situation that needs to be corrected, something that needs to come to an end, or it may be a prayer assignment for a person's salvation.

Death in a dream may be signaling the end, "death," or correction of:

- a sin or other habit that needs to end;

- a lie that you believed could be exposed and ended;

- a relationship that is changing or ending;

- double-mindedness or a heart that is not secure in Jesus;

- the end of selfish ways, refusing to demand your own way anymore (Matthew 10:38);

- a shift—the end of the old life or old pattern, and the new mindset and joy-filled life is on the way.

1. Read Romans 8:6. What is the difference between the mind set on the flesh and the mind set on the spirit?

_____

_____

_____

_____

_____

_____

_____

2. Which of these six "deaths" listed above are applicable to your current situation?

_____

_____

_____

_____

_____

_____

_____

Your own heart, will, or desires can influence a dream. Without realizing it, your own heart may be the problem God wants to help you understand. Our selfish tendencies to *get our own way,* may influence our dreams or the interpretation. When we give God permission to change our heart, He works to accomplish this even in our sleep.

1. Read and write a paraphrase of Jeremiah 17:9.

   _____

   _____

   _____

   _____

   _____

   _____

   _____

2. Write Psalm 127:2 from the Amplified version of the Bible.

   _____

   _____

   _____

   _____

   _____

   _____

   _____

Daniel, Hananiah, Mishael, and Azariah, though young, had uncommon boldness and wisdom. Remember: When you love God, you have access to the same wisdom, intelligence, and brilliance that Daniel and his friends had. When we read, listen to, and memorize the Word, we will better understand dreams, mysteries and parables.

1. What gifts did God give Daniel, Hananiah, Mishael, and Azariah? (Daniel 1:17-19)

_____

_____

_____

_____

2. In addition to saving their lives, what was the result of Daniel interpreting the king's dream? (Daniel 2:46-49)

_____

_____

_____

_____

_____

_____

_____

_____

The Hebrew word for *knowledge* here is *madda,* which carries the meaning of God's intelligence or knowledge and understanding His presence. These young men were seriously obedient to God no matter what the circumstances (remember the lion's den and fiery furnace). In this obedience and faithfulness, God accelerated their ability to understand His thoughts and increased their depth of wisdom, and Nebuchadnezzar elevated them in government.

1. Would you have chosen to go into the fiery furnace or would you have bowed down?

_____

_____

_____

_____

_____

2. What challenging future decisions are on your horizon that you need God's wisdom for? Ask Him to speak to you about them in a dream.

_____

_____

_____

_____

_____

_____

_____

_____

_____

_____

_____

_____

_____

_____

_____

_____

_____

_____

You can be bold because you are a child of the Most High God, King of the ultimate Kingdom! Under the New Covenant you have bold access to the Throne of God and His justice. As part of the chosen generation, you live under a blessing covering. God has given you the mind of Christ—He is for you, never against you! You are highly favored, holy, and He and His life is increasing in you daily. You are seated with Him and share His authority.

1. Write two scriptures that confirm your standing with God.

_____

_____

_____

_____

_____

_____

_____

_____

2. What does it mean to have the mind of Christ? (See 1 Corinthians 2:16.)

_____

_____

_____

_____

In closing out this journal, I pray you have dreams, dreams, and more dreams, along with the Lord's wisdom for interpretation and application to your life. I also wish you the determination it takes to follow through with all that is required in the process of interpreting and applying your dreams.

1. Write your thoughts about what you have learned through this process.

_____

_____

_____

_____

_____

_____

_____

_____

_____

_____

_____

_____

_____

_____

_____

_____

_____

_____

2. Write a prayer of thanks to the Lord for leading you and giving you revelation.

_____

_____

_____

_____

_____

_____

_____

_____

_____

_____

_____

_____

_____

_____

_____

_____

_____

_____

A NOTE TO PARENTS

I encourage you to train young believers in understanding their dreams. Draw them into the learning process and gently compel them not only to read but to dwell on the Word of God. This will give excellent understanding and open up brilliant revelation in their own dreams with Holy Spirit's guidance. As God's Word is sown into their heart and mind, they will come to understand His love and good plans for them. His excellence and truth will become their high standard and they will never be compelled or satisfied by an inferior or unrighteous source. Statistics are abysmal of Christian youth who hit college and then turn from the faith. My prayer is that every child of God will continually crave the living, breathing, vibrant, and healthy food of God's Word they've been blessed to feast on. Once they've encountered Jesus and His power, they'll never be content with less than another encounter of His love.

SUGGESTED DREAM RESOURCES

Dictionary of Biblical Imagery by Leland Ryken

Dream Language by Jim & Michal Ann Goll

Invitation to Encounter by Julie Miller

The Name Book by Dorothy Astoria

Understanding the Dreams that you Dream by Ira Milligan

Unlocking Dreams Student Manual by John Paul Jackson

NOTES

1. John Paul Jackson, "Dreams By John Paul Jackson," 2020, https://archive.org/details/dreams-by-john-paul-jackson (accessed 4-2-22).

2. John Paul Jackson, "DREAMS – John Paul Jackson," 2021, https://4jesus.site/2021/09/20/dreams-john-paul-jackson/ (accessed 4-2-22).

3. Ibid.

4. Adam F. Thompson and Adrian Beale, qtd. in *The Dream Book,* Stephanie Schureman, "Foreword."

5. John Paul Jackson, "Dreams By John Paul Jackson," 2020, https://archive.org/details/dreams-by-john-paul-jackson (accessed 4-2-22).

6. John Paul Jackson was an American author, teacher, conference speaker and founder of Streams Ministries International. Jackson often focused on supernatural topics like dreams, visions, and dream interpretation as found in the Bible.

7. John Paul Jackson, "DREAMS – John Paul Jackson," 2021, https://4jesus.site/2021/09/20/dreams-john-paul-jackson/ (accessed 4-2-22).

8. Ibid.

9. John Paul Jackson, "Unlocking Your Dreams Course & Manual," n.d., http://www.unlockingyourdreams.org/StudentManual.pdf (date accessed 4-2-22).

10. John Paul Jackson, "Dreams By John Paul Jackson," 2020, https://archive.org/details/dreams-by-john-paul-jackson (accessed 4-2-22).

11. Lou Engle, n.d., https://louengle.com/ (date accessed 4-3-22).

12. John Paul Jackson, "Unlocking Your Dreams Course & Manual," n.d., http://www.unlockingyourdreams.org/ StudentManual.pdf (date accessed 4-2-22).

13. John Paul Jackson, "Unlocking Your Dreams Course & Manual," n.d., http://www.unlockingyourdreams.org/ StudentManual.pdf (date accessed 4-2-22).

ABOUT STEPHANIE SCHUREMAN

Stephanie Schureman is an author, speaker, and founding pastor of Dwelling Place Ministry. She has written two books: *Here I Am, the One You Love* and *The Dream Book: A Beginner's Guide to Understanding God's Voice When You Sleep*. Stephanie is a homeschooling mother of 6 children, blessed with 6 grandchildren (and counting), and wife of Cris for over 38 years. They reside in Golden, Colorado.

YOUR

Prophetic

COMMUNITY

Are you passionate about hearing God's voice, walking with Jesus, and experiencing the power of the Holy Spirit?

Destiny Image is a community of believers with a passion for equipping and encouraging you to live the prophetic, supernatural life you were created for!

We offer a fresh helping of practical articles, dynamic podcasts, and powerful videos from respected, Spirit-empowered, Christian leaders to fuel the holy fire within you.

Sign up now to get awesome content delivered to your inbox
destinyimage.com/sign-up

 Destiny Image